PICKUP TRUCKS

RYAN EARLEY

MIGHTY TRUCKS

TABLE OF CONTENTS

A Pelican Book

SEAHORSE PUBLISHING

Teaching Tips for Caregivers and Teachers:

Research shows that one of the best ways for students to learn a new topic is to read about it.

Before Reading

- Read the title and predict what the book will be about.
- Read the "Words to Know" and discuss the meaning of each word.
- Read the back cover to see what the book is about.

During Reading

- When a student gets to a word that is unknown, ask them to look at the rest of the sentence to find clues to help with the meaning of the unknown word.
- Motivate students with praise and encouragement.

After Reading

- Discuss the main idea of the book.
- Ask students to give one detail that they learned in the book.

Sight Words

a
all
are
big
four
have
is
most
some
this

Words to Know

cab

hitch

pickup truck

tailgate

wheels

This is a **pickup truck.**

pickup truck

All pickup trucks have four **wheels**.

wheel
4MOTION
V6 TDI
AROK
ZG 8612-GG

All pickup trucks have a **cab**.

cab

Most pickup trucks have a **tailgate**.

tailgate

Some pickup trucks have a **hitch**.

Some pickup trucks are big!

Index

Written by: Ryan Earley
Design by: Savina Magaro
Editor: Kim Thompson
Series Development: James Earley

Photos: Ford Motor Co.: cover; Jake Steele: p. 5; supergenijalac: p. 7; stockfoundation: p. 9; toiletroom: p. 11; Patnaree: p. 12-13; Brad Sauter: p. 15

Library of Congress PCN Data
Pickup Trucks / Ryan Earley
Mighty Trucks
ISBN 978-1-6389-7950-0(hard cover)
ISBN 979-8-8873-5009-7(paperback)
ISBN 979-8-8873-5068-4(EPUB)
ISBN 979-8-8873-5127-8(eBook)
Library of Congress Control Number: 2022942270
Printed in the United States of America.

Seahorse Publishing Company
seahorsepub.com 1-800-387-7650

Published in the United States
Seahorse Publishing
PO Box 771325
Coral Springs, FL 33077

SEAHORSE PUBLISHING